KU-394-429

Garfield

A Weekend AWAY

BY: JIM DAVIS

RAVETTE BOOKS

COPYRIGHT © 1986 United Feature Syndicate, Inc.
All Rights Reserved.
GARFIELD Comic Strips: © 1979, 1980, 1981, 1982, 1983, 1984.
United Feature Syndicate, Inc. All Rights Reserved

This edition first published by Ravette Books Limited 1988.

This book is sold subject to the condition that it shall not, by way of
trade or otherwise, be lent, re-sold, hired out or otherwise circulated
without the publisher's prior consent in any form of binding or cover
other than that in which this is published and without a similar
condition including this condition being imposed on the subsequent
purchaser.

Printed and bound for Ravette Books Limited,
3 Glenside Estate, Star Road,
Partridge Green, Horsham,
Sussex RH13 8RA
by Purnell Book Production Limited
Paulton, Bristol
A member of BPCC plc

ISBN: 1 85304 062 2

Garfield

Pack up your troubles and fly away with Garfield to a relaxing holiday resort for the weekend. No weekend away is complete without a good supply of holiday humour courtesy of Garfield. Whether you're camping, skiing, at the beach, on the farm or just getting away from it all, Garfield makes the ideal travelling companion.

Don't leave home without him!

LOOK OUT, SUNNY BEACHES

8-18

© 1981 United Feature Syndicate, Inc.

HERE COMES DON JUAN

JIM DAVIS

AND HIS SIDEKICK, LAWRENCE OF BOXER SHORTS

Down Hill Racer.

HMMM, JON'S DRAWING BOARD. HMMM, SOME PAPER. HMMM, SOME INK

I THINK THIS WORLD WOULD BE A NICER PLACE IN WHICH TO LIVE: IF COUNTRIES COULD SETTLE THEIR DIFFERENCES WITHOUT HURTING ANYBODY. IF EVERYONE SMILED AT EVEN PEOPLE THEY DIDN'T KNOW

IF NOBODY HAD TO STEAL. IF PEOPLE LAUGHED MORE. IF EVERYONE FED THEIR CATS ALL THE LASAGNA THEY COULD EAT. IF WE ALL TOOK MORE PRIDE IN OUR HOMES AND OUR NEIGHBORHOODS

3-18

© 1979 United Feature Syndicate, Inc

IF WE RESPECTED OUR SENIOR CITIZENS MORE. IF THERE WERE NO VIOLENCE IN MOVIES AND TELEVISION. IF EVERYONE COULD READ AND WRITE. IF FAMILIES TALKED MORE

IF FRIENDS HUGGED MORE. IF EVERYONE STOPPED AT LEAST ONCE A WEEK TO STROKE A CAT. AFTER ALL, WE'RE ALL IN THIS TOGETHER

HEY, GARFIELD

WHAT'S THIS?

OH, JUST SOME PAW PRINTS

JIM DAVIS

3-25

© 1979 United Feature Syndicate, Inc.

SIGH

HO HUM

GARFIELD

EVER HAD ONE OF THOSE DAYS WHEN YOU FEEL LIKE YOU'VE SLEPT AND EATEN IT ALL?

JIM DAVIS

Perfect Co-ordination.

Is it a bird? Is it a plane? No it's, it's...

CLICK

I'M GOING TO STARE AT THIS TOASTER UNTIL THE TOAST POPS UP

A WATCHED POT NEVER BOILS, GARFIELD

HUH?

POP

© 1979 United Feature Syndicate, Inc.

SEE?

DRAT... DRAT, DRAT, DRAT, DRAT

JIM DAVIS

4-8

GROWL

THE CAT CRAVES FRESH MEAT

4-29

WHAT-HO, THE CAT SENSES UNSUSPECTING QUARRY O'ER YON KNOLL

© 1979 United Feature Syndicate, Inc.

JIM DAVIS

COILING LIKE A SPRING, HE PREPARES TO LUNGE

STEELY SINEWS PROPEL HIM TOWARD HIS HELPLESS PREY

ONCE AGAIN A CAT'S PRIMAL INSTINCTS PROVIDE SUSTENANCE

Too deer for me...

PURRRR

PURRR

TAPPITY
TAPPITY
TAPPITY

TAPPITY
TAPPITY
TAPPITY

5-6

SCRATCH!
SCRATCH!
SCRATCH!
SCRATCH!

GOOD MORNING, SUNSHINE. WELCOME TO ANOTHER GLORIOUS, FUN-FILLED DAY WITH YOUR FAVORITE PET!

I'M SO HAPPY TO OWN A CAT, I COULD JUST THROW UP

JIM DAVIS

Room for Improvement.

JIM DAVIS

Dropping in on a friend...

JIM DAVIS

I'm turning over a new leaf.

JIM DAVIS

Let's hope it's a 4 leaf-clover.

7-29

© 1979 United Feature Syndicate, Inc.

JIM DAVIS

wake me when
this fitness fad
is over

JIM DAVIS

© 1979 United Feature Syndicate, Inc.

CARTOONIST'S NOTE:
TODAY'S GARFIELD STRIP IS TO BE READ ONLY BY FAT PEOPLE, OR PEOPLE WITH FAT TENDENCIES. YOU SKINNY ONES CAN READ THE OTHER STRIPS, OR JOG, OR DRINK A GLASS OF WATER, OR WHATEVER IT IS SKINNY PEOPLE DO. ...I WOULDN'T KNOW.

I AM HEREBY DECLARING THIS COMING WEEK, "NATIONAL FAT WEEK"

OUT OF THE CLOSET, YOU FATTIES!

THIS WEEK WE'RE GOING TO EAT WITHOUT GUILT

9-23

REMEMBER OUR SLOGAN: "IF IT'S NOT DEEP-FRIED, IT'S NOT WORTH EATING."

WE'LL BOYCOTT CARROTS AND TELL SKINNY JOKES

I WOULD HAVE HAD A NATIONAL CONVENTION

BUT I COULDN'T GET THE KANSAS CITY STOCKYARDS TO CATER IT

JIM DAVIS

Ex rcising my right to object!

CRASH!

GARFIELD! YOU BROKE MY FERN!!

© 1979 United Feature Syndicate, Inc.

I RAISED THAT FERN FROM A FROND!

12-30

WHAT DID THAT FERN EVER DO TO YOU?!!

WHY, I HAVE A NOTION TO...UH...TO

I...UH

YOU'RE SO CUTE

LIKE PUTTY IN MY PAWS

JIM DAVIS

This fitness craze will be the death of me.

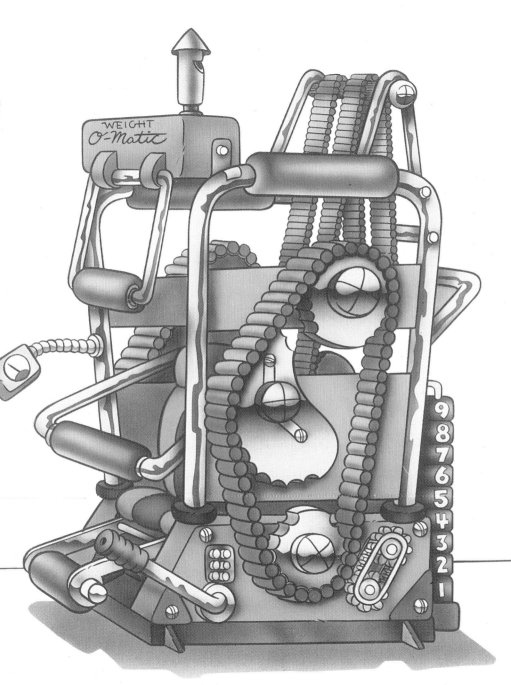

BACK OFF, GARFIELD. THAT TURKEY LEG IS FOR MY LUNCH

AHCHOO!

WIPE
WIPE
WIPE
WIPE

SCRATCH
SCRATCH
SCRATCH
SCRATCH
SCRATCH
SCRATCH

© 1980 United Feature Syndicate, Inc   1-6

WOULD YOU LIKE A TURKEY LEG, GARFIELD?

ONLY IF YOU DON'T WANT IT

JIM DAVIS

I THOUGHT SO

© 1980 United Feature Syndicate, Inc

JIM DAVIS

1-13

OH BOY IS IT CHILLY THIS MORNING

SPLASH SPLASH SPLASH

SIP

GARGLE GARGLE GARGLE

© 1980 United Feature Syndicate, Inc

GULP

THAT FEELS SO WARM

AHHH

YOU REALLY ENJOY YOUR COFFEE, DON'T YOU, GARFIELD?

JIM DAVIS

2-3

"How did I get into this mess?"

JIM DAVIS

WATCH THIS. I'M GOING TO SWING DOWN ON THIS VINE AND SWOOP UP JON'S CHICKEN

YANK YANK

SWOOP!

JIM DAVIS

WHERE DID THE VINE COME FROM?

© 1980 United Feature Syndicate, Inc

2-10

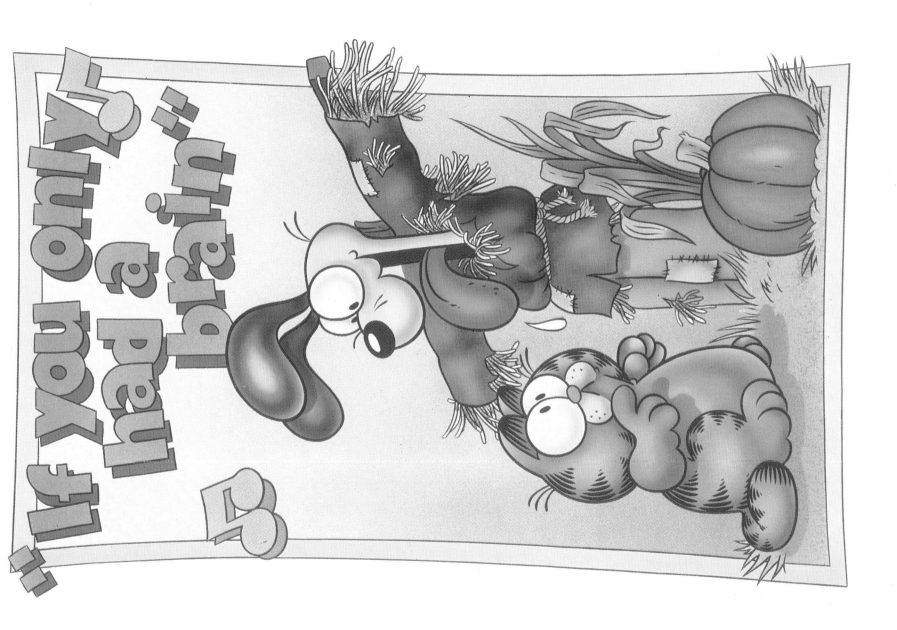

© 1980 United Feature Syndicate Inc

3-16

ZIP!

WHERE THERE'S A WILL...

JIM DAVIS

HEY, GARFIELD. LET'S GO JOGGING

SHOOP

© 1980 United Feature Syndicate, Inc.

JIM DAVIS

AHA!

EEEYOUCH!

SWIPE

11-16

THIS IS ONE OF THOSE TIMES WHEN I SHOULD HAVE CONSIDERED THE CONSEQUENCES OF MY ACTIONS

JiM DAViS

"Odie is my only Handicap."

© 1980 United Feature Syndicate, Inc.

JIM DAVIS

11-23

HELLO? FUNNY FARM? DO YOU TAKE PETS?

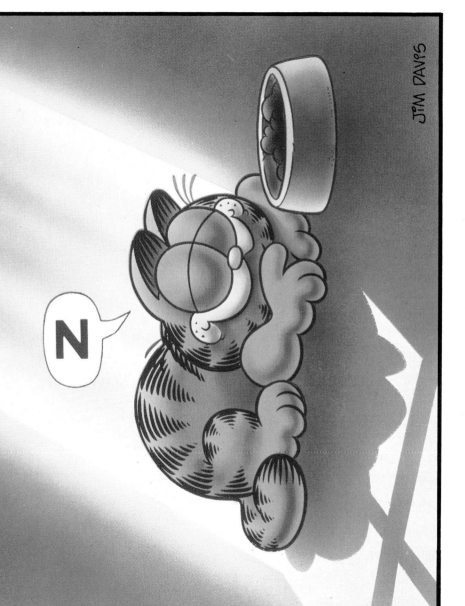

Working in the Garden.

"A Bright Star."

JiM DaViS

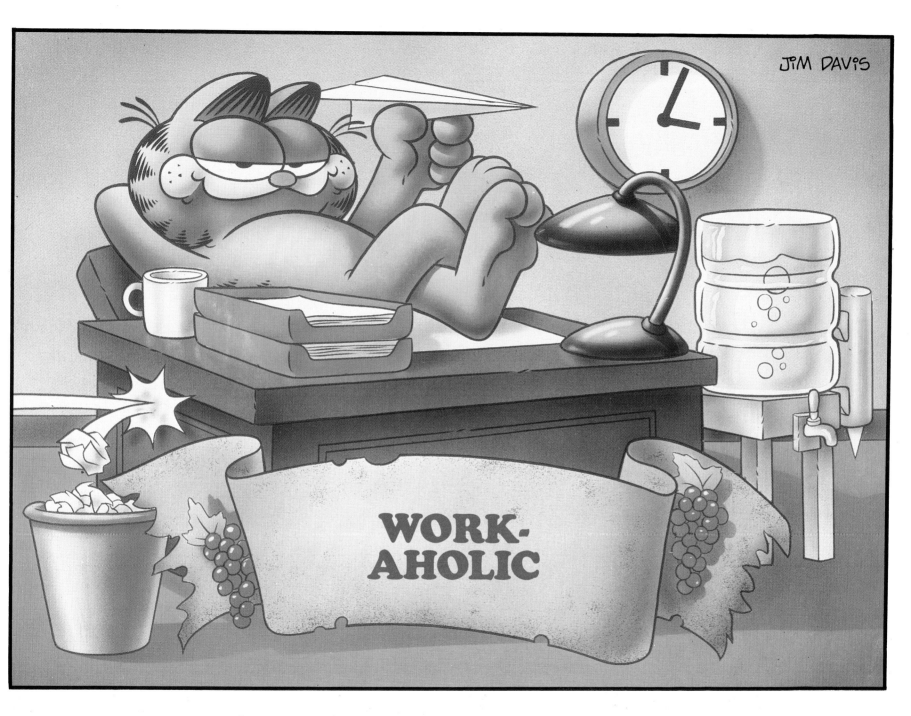

All work and no pay...

© 1981 United Feature Syndicate Inc

I'm the "Rugged Indoor Type."

WHY, HELLO THERE

I'M LOST

AREN'T YOU CUTE!

CAN YOU GIVE ME DIRECTIONS?

2-1

RUN ALONG NOW, KITTY

WHAT DID I DO?

JIM DAVIS

© 1981 United Feature Syndicate, Inc.

2-8

JIM DAVIS

© 1981 United Feature Syndicate, Inc

Why me?

Why not!

JIM DAVIS

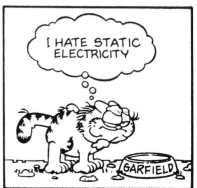

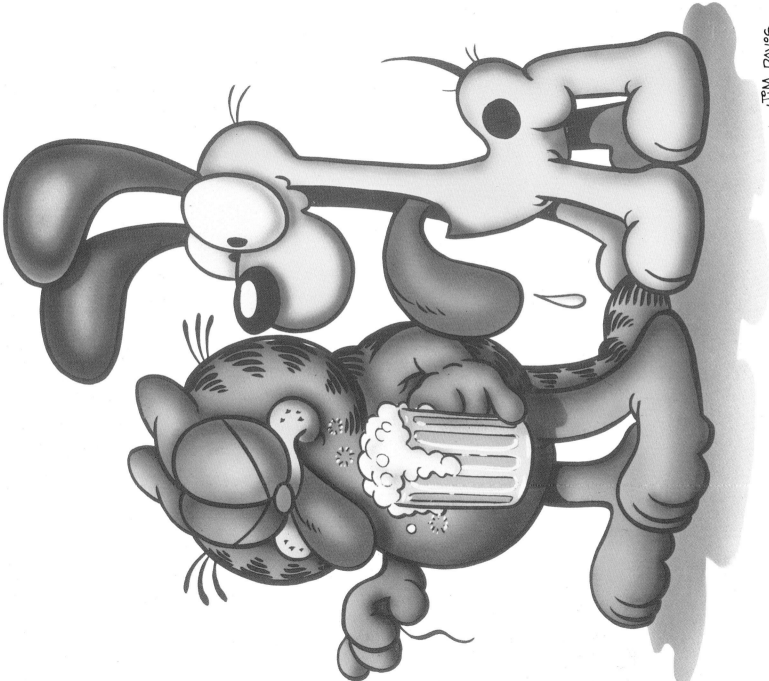

"Hair of the Dog," yuk!

JIM DAVIS

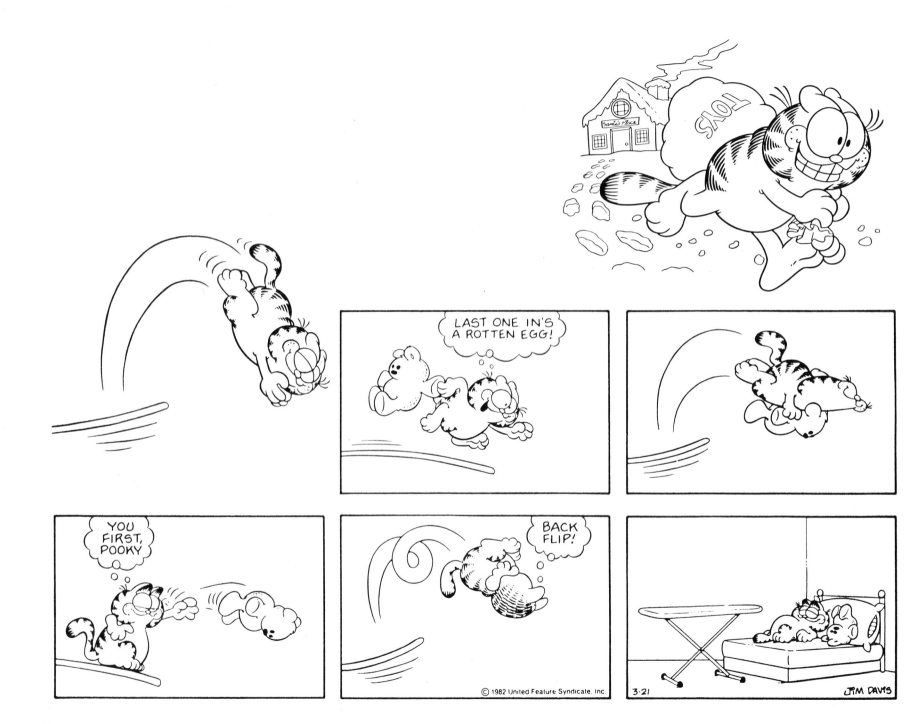

I'M GOING TO JOG THIS MORNING

3-22   JIM DAVIS

OF COURSE, IT WILL BE COLD WHEN I START

BUT, THEN I'LL GET HOT AND SWEATY

AND MY HEART WILL POUND, MAKING ME DIZZY

I'LL GET BLISTERS ON MY FEET

THEN I'LL BE STIFF AND SORE FOR DAYS

JOGGING PROBABLY WOULDN'T BE SO BAD. BUT THE ANTICIPATION IS KILLING ME

© 1981 United Feature Syndicate, Inc.

Garfield takes the cake!

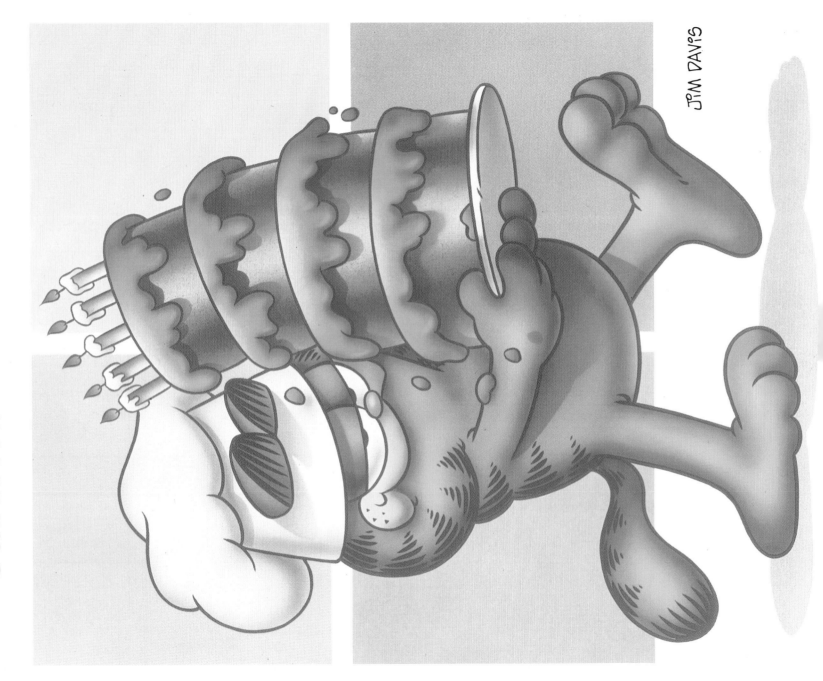

JIM DAVIS

© 1983 United Feature Syndicate, Inc.

My FUR-tive Imagination at work.

JIM DAVIS

So long...I'll catch you later...You'all come back soon now, y'hear!